D1252631

TOY STORY 4

THE SECRET SCIENCE OF TOYS

A Toy Story Discovery Book

By Kris Hirschmann

Special thanks to Professor Suveen N. Mathaudhu,
University of California, Riverside

Lerner Publications Company
An imprint of Lerner Publishing Group, Inc.
241 First Avenue North
Minneapolis, MN 55401 USA

For reading levels and more information, look up this title at www.lernerbooks.com.

Main body text set in Mikado 12/20.
Typeface provided by HVD Fonts.

Library of Congress Cataloging-in-Publication Data

Names: Hirschmann, Kris, 1967- author. | Disney Enterprises (1996-) | Disney Storybook Artists, illustrator.
Title: The secret science of toys : a Toy Story discovery book / Kris Hirschmann.
Description: Minneapolis, MN : Lerner Publications Company, [2019] | Series: Disney learning discovery books | Audience: Ages 7–11. | Audience: Grades 4 to 6. | Includes index.
Identifiers: LCCN 2019016300 (print) | LCCN 2019019214 (ebook) | ISBN 9781541561441 (eb pdf) | ISBN 9781541554900 (lb : alk. paper) | ISBN 9781541573918 (pb : alk. paper)
Subjects: LCSH: Toys—Juvenile literature. | Toy making—Juvenile literature. | Toys—History—Juvenile literature. | Toy story films—Juvenile literature.
Classification: LCC TT174 (ebook) | LCC TT174 .H57 2019 (print) | DDC 688.7/2—dc23

LC record available at https://lccn.loc.gov/2019016300

Manufactured in the United States of America
1-45808-42690-4/17/2019

CONTENTS

IT'S PLAYTIME!

Forky is Bonnie's toy, but what exactly is a toy? It is any object that gets played with! Many toys are designed on purpose for this use. Others are just random objects, like rocks, sticks, or spoons, that are turned into toys by the power of a child's imagination. Most importantly, whatever its shape, size, or origin, a toy is FUN!

But guess what? It's not just fun. All toys—yes, ALL—operate on scientific principles. Bouncing? That's science. Flashing? That's science too. Walking, talking, and driving? Science, science, science . . . and this book will show you how it all works. Read on to discover the secret science of toys!

ANCIENT TOYS

Woody and Gabby Gabby were made in the 1950s, but there are toys much older than that. Children have been playing with toys since the dawn of humankind. Ancient toys were made from any materials that were handy. These toys were simple, but they were still full of science! They helped children understand the way the world worked.

Built from Scratch

Long before dolls were made from fabric, children were assembling them from natural objects. Corn-husk dolls, for example, were made from sticks and corn husks tied together. Corny, but lovable!

Corn-husk dolls

Figure made from acorns and matchsticks

Sticks and Rocks

According to the National Toy Hall of Fame, the humble stick is the oldest toy. But rocks can't be far behind! Sticks and rocks are used for building, as bats and balls, as a springboard for imaginary play, and in countless other ways. Grab a stick and a rock. Move them around, feel them, and experiment with them. Everything you observe is science in action.

Clay Toys

Long ago, children molded dolls, animals, and other toys from clay. The damp clay hardened as its moisture **evaporated**. The dry clay held its shape.

TOYS THROUGH THE AGES

Mr. Potato Head was first manufactured in the early 1950s. The toy was originally just a set of plastic parts with pushpins. Kids stuck the parts into a real potato or other vegetable. A plastic potato was first included in the kit in 1964. Through the ages, people learned how to harness natural and **synthetic** materials and forces to make more complicated things. Toys got more sophisticated!

Porcelain Faces

The term *china doll* refers to dolls with shiny **porcelain** heads and body parts. Bo Peep is made from porcelain. Porcelain is a **ceramic**. It is made by heating clay containing a material called **kaolin** to temperatures of about 2,600°F (1,425°C) in a **kiln**. The technique came from China around twelve hundred years ago and slowly spread around the world. Most antique china dolls come from Germany, which had a booming doll industry in the mid to late nineteenth century.

Mechanical Marvels

Mechanical toys like Lenny and Tinny have been popular for nearly twenty-five hundred years. They work by transforming **energy** from one source, like a crank or a spring, into movement. Their inner parts include levers, pulleys, wheels and **axles**, planes, wedges, and screws—the six devices known as **simple machines**. Simple machines change forces in ways that make work easier.

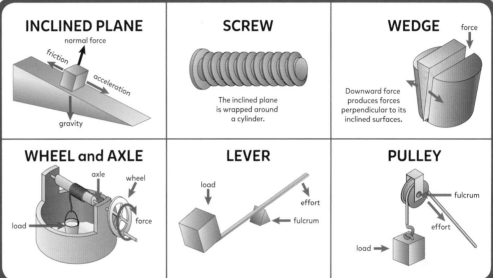

INCLINED PLANE
normal force
friction
acceleration
gravity

SCREW
The inclined plane is wrapped around a cylinder.

WEDGE
force
Downward force produces forces perpendicular to its inclined surfaces.

WHEEL and AXLE
axle
wheel
load
force

LEVER
load
effort
fulcrum

PULLEY
fulcrum
effort
load

Sewn with Love

Around 34,000 BCE, **textiles** were developed. Textiles are flexible materials made of a network of **fibers**. Fabric and cloth (processed fabric) are textiles. These materials can be cut or torn into the needed shape, then sewn back together with needle and thread. The earliest cloth dolls probably appeared soon after clothing did! Dolly is a good example of a cloth doll.

WOODEN TOYS

Most of Andy's toys were plastic—except maybe his blocks. In ancient times, children played with hand-carved wooden toys. Between about 1760 and 1830, however, a period called the Industrial Revolution changed everything! People learned how to use machines and automation to make many things, including wooden toys.

Factory Made

In factories, machines and people work together to create toys. Machines do most of the preliminary work. They cut, shape, sand, and paint wooden parts. People are often needed to **assemble** some or all of the parts. They may also paint fine details onto the finished toys.

Painting a wooden top

Wood-engraving machine

Nesting Dolls

The wooden nesting doll, or *matryoshka*, originated in Russia. These dolls were once made and painted entirely by hand. Today machines help people shape, sand, paint, and varnish the dolls. But still, each set must be made from the same piece of wood. Why? Wood expands or swells and shrinks depending on the amount of moisture in the air. When the air is damp, the wood swells; when it is dry, the wood shrinks. When one piece of wood is used, all the dolls in the set swell and shrink in the same way. If different pieces of wood were used, the pieces wouldn't nest correctly!

Squished Sawdust

Sawdust can be shaped into parts for toys! The sawdust is dyed, and a tiny bit of glue is added. The mixture is then pressed into **molds**. When the glue dries, the finished object has the look and feel of real wood. This process lets manufacturers make complex shapes without carving anything.

TAKING SHAPE

Many modern toys like Combat Carl and Giggle McDimples are molded. This means they start out as soft or melted material. They are shaped and hardened using techniques that combine temperature, **pressure**, and other scientific principles.

Plastic toys being produced at a factory

Injection Molding

Injection molding is a process by which **molten** plastic is injected into a hollow mold. The plastic cools and hardens very quickly, often within seconds. The finished object is ejected from the mold. Then new plastic is injected. An injection molding machine can quickly turn out thousands of identical objects—such as toy soldiers!

Compression Molding

A process called **compression** molding shapes plastic by squeezing it. Molten plastic is poured into a mold, then pressed from both sides. The plastic cools and hardens into a thin layer that is shaped like the mold. This technique is great for making dinosaur skin, potato heads, and other hard plastic pieces.

Die-casting

Die-casting is like injection molding, but it uses molten metal instead of plastic. In the toy industry, die-casting is most commonly used for making scale models of cars, airplanes, and other vehicles. It is also used to make Monopoly game pieces, such as the racing car, top hat, and dog.

Die-cast car

Mold for tin soldiers

Classic Monopoly game pieces

WINDUP TOYS

Windup toys like Lenny have a type of **clockwork** mechanism. They all work on the same general principle. A person winds the toy. The toy then moves in various ways, depending on its design. How does it happen? Let's find out!

Energy Transfer

Energy transfer is the conversion of one form of energy to another, or the movement of energy from one place to another. For windup toys, a person tightens a metal coil called a **mainspring**. The person must exert energy to make this happen. The mainspring stores this energy in the form of **potential energy**. It releases the energy as it unwinds and turns it into movement, which is also called **kinetic energy**.

Mainspring

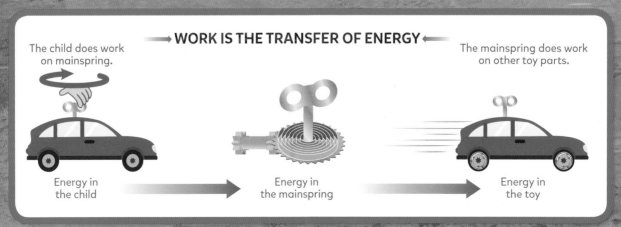

➤ **WORK IS THE TRANSFER OF ENERGY** ◄

The child does work on mainspring.

The mainspring does work on other toy parts.

Energy in the child → Energy in the mainspring → Energy in the toy

Windup mechanism

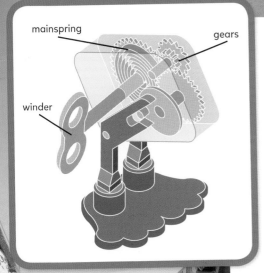

mainspring

gears

winder

Hopping Along

Windup hopping toys are trickier than you'd think! Inside these toys, the mainspring drives a system of gears, wheels, and pins that spin around and push one another in complicated ways. The final component is a wheel that advances one notch at a time. Each time the wheel clicks forward, it pushes the toy's little feet. Hop, hop, hop!

Pullback Vehicle

A pullback vehicle like Duke Caboom is a variation of a windup toy. Instead of winding a knob, a person makes the car's wheels rotate. The toy stores this energy in a mainspring, just as other windup toys do. As the energy is released, ZOOM! The car zips forward!

BATTERY POWER

Many toys draw power from **batteries**. Batteries, also called **cells**, are electrical power packs that can produce **electricity** whenever and wherever it is needed. Like mainsprings, batteries store potential energy, but in a chemical rather than mechanical form. When released, this energy is transformed into movement, light, or sound.

How Batteries Work

Today there are many types of batteries. The old-fashioned types—like the ones labeled AA, AAA, C, and D—are full of a chemical called an **electrolyte**. Each end of the battery has a terminal. One terminal, called the **anode**, likes to give up negatively charged **particles** called **electrons**. The other terminal, called the **cathode**, likes to receive electrons. When the terminals are connected, the action happens! The electrolyte starts to release electrons, which flow from one terminal to another. This movement is an electrical **current**.

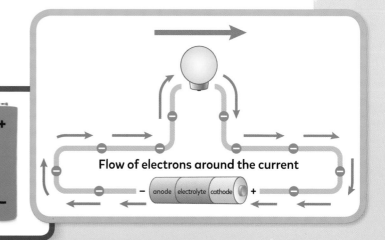

Flow of electrons around the current

anode electrolyte cathode

Light It Up

When Buzz Lightyear presses a button on his arm, a "laser beam" fires with sound and light. A battery powers this feature. Pressing the button closes a **circuit**, which is a pathway from one of the battery's terminals to the other. Electrons flow and the laser beam turns on. When the button is released, the circuit is broken. The flow of electricity stops, and the laser beam turns off.

Making It Go

In battery-powered cars like RC, chemical potential energy turns into kinetic mechanical energy. It's not a direct transfer. It's a three-step process where chemical energy turns into electrical energy, which mechanically drives a motor. This creates a **magnetic** field. The magnetic field makes a pole called a driveshaft rotate, and this motion powers the car. *Ba-da-boom*—movement!

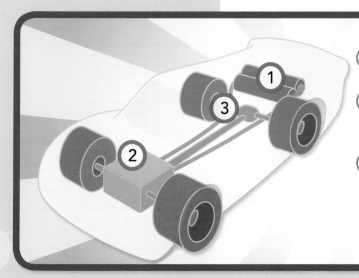

1. Batteries turn chemical potential energy into electrical energy.

2. Electrical energy drives a motor. Spinning parts in the motor create a magnetic field.

3. The magnetic field makes a driveshaft spin. Motion from the driveshaft is transferred to other parts of the car by gears. The wheels spin, and the car moves.

BUILDING TOYS

Building toys let kids exercise their creativity and experiment with **forces** at the same time. Let's take a look at the science of toy construction.

What Is a Force?

Push →   Pull →

Before we start to talk about forces, let's define them! In scientific terms, a force is a push or pull upon an object. Forces are defined by their **magnitude**, which means their strength, and their direction. Forces can make objects change their speed or direction.

Construction Toys

Some popular construction toys are like bricks that snap together. Others have rods that are inserted into joining pieces with holes. Both types of toys work through a combination of pressure (a constant pushing force) and **friction** (a force that controls how easily two surfaces slide against each other). These forces work together to hold the pieces in place.

Joints

When two parts are connected in a way that lets them move relative to each other, the meeting point is called a **joint**. The human body has joints where the bones meet. How many moving joints can you identify on your body? Count them and see!

Potato Heads

Mr. and Mrs. Potato Head are variations on a construction toy. Each add-on piece has a peg that is pushed into a hole in the central potato body. The pegs fit tightly into the holes. The pressure increases the friction that holds the pegs in place. When you pull on a piece, you provide enough force to overcome the friction and pressure, and the peg slides out.

TOYS IN MOTION

Anything that moves—including toys—can be an endless source of scientific discussion. Let's look at some topics that apply to toys in motion.

Play = Work

When scientists use the word **work**, they don't mean going to a job. In scientific terms, *work* means "using a force to move an object." So when you push or pull moving toys, or even pick them up, you're doing work . . . according to scientists, anyway!

Loop the Loop

When a toy car loops the loop, why doesn't it fall down? A bunch of things come into play here. At the top of the loop, a force called **gravity** is pulling the car downward. But at the same time, the car's forward motion around a curved loop creates something called a **centrifugal force**. This force keeps the car and track against each other. The greater the speed, the greater the centrifugal force. If the centrifugal force is stronger than gravity, ta-da! The car loops the loop!

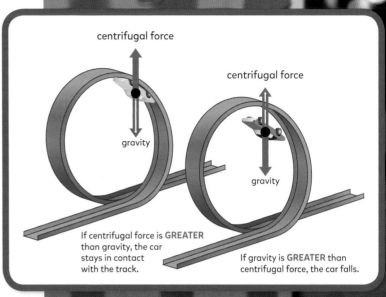

centrifugal force

gravity

centrifugal force

gravity

If centrifugal force is GREATER than gravity, the car stays in contact with the track.

If gravity is GREATER than centrifugal force, the car falls.

Karate-Chop Action

What is the science behind Buzz's karate-chop action? It has to do with a basic law of motion: an object at rest will stay at rest unless acted upon by an external force. Most of the time, Buzz's arm doesn't move. When a button is pressed, however, a hidden mechanism inside Buzz's body pushes his forearm. This external force shoves Buzz's forearm forward. Chop, chop! The same principle applies to whatever Buzz's arm hits. The object is stationary until Buzz karate-chops it. Then it goes flying—or breaking, if it happens to be a pile of bricks!

NOISEMAKERS

Toys like the squeaky toy aliens and noise go together! Listen up and learn about what's happening when your toys squeak, chat, or make other sounds.

Squeak!

Poor Wheezy the penguin has a broken squeaker, so he can't squeak properly. If his squeaker did work, though, here's what it would do. Toy squeakers have small holes covered or lined with flexible plastic. When you squeeze the toy, air is forced through the hole. The airflow makes the plastic vibrate rapidly, and this **vibration** creates the sound we hear.

Talk Boxes

Dolls like Woody and Gabby Gabby have a talking mechanism that is activated by a pull-string. Pulling the string turns a tiny record inside the doll's body. Some newer pull-string dolls also have mechanical talk boxes hidden inside their bodies. When the string is pulled, metal plates inside the talk box bend to touch one another. This completes a circuit and activates a battery. The battery in turn activates a small audio storage device, which sends a recorded message to a speaker.

Hearing

Our sense of hearing lets us listen to the sounds our toys make. Sounds travel through the air as vibrations. These vibrations enter the ear and hit a **membrane** called the eardrum. The eardrum vibrates like the skin of a drum. Nerves carry information about these vibrations to the brain, which interprets the signals as sounds.

outer ear   middle ear   inner ear

1. Sound starts.
2. Sound travels through the air as vibrations.
3. The eardrum vibrates.
4. Nerves carry information to the brain.

23

SPRINGS AND THINGS

Slinky toys like Woody's faithful friend, Slinky Dog, have been fascinating children and adults alike since they were invented in the mid twentieth century. These stretching, stair-stepping devices aren't just fun—they are classic examples of science in action.

Springs

The classic metal Slinky is a type of spring. Metal springs are **elastic**. This means they may bend or stretch if forced, but they will tend to return to their original shape—unless you bend them too far! Then they may be permanently changed. Changing a spring's shape, either temporarily or permanently, requires work and creates potential energy. The spring's shift back to its original form is movement, or kinetic energy.

Walking Down Stairs

Why does a Slinky walk down stairs? When the Slinky is bent to place one end on a lower stair, gravity pulls on the toy. This pull stretches the spring little by little. The top end stays put—for a while, anyway. At some point, the pull of gravity yanks the top end off its stair. The end flips with enough force to carry it over and forward, and it tumbles down the next step. The whole process repeats until the Slinky reaches the bottom of the stairs.

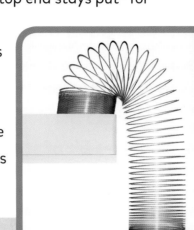

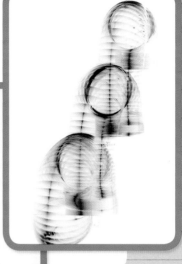

Accidental Invention

The Slinky was not designed as a toy. It was created by engineer Richard James in 1943 as a spring meant to **stabilize** instruments on ships in rough seas. It didn't work well for its intended use, so James decided to market it as a toy . . . and one of history's most successful playthings was born!

LOOK WHO'S TALKING

Ventriloquists are performers who seem to "throw" their voices into dolls like Benson known as **dummies.** The ventriloquist's mouth doesn't appear to move—yet somehow the dummy talks. Let's take a closer look at this bit of stage magic!

Throwing Your Voice

How does a ventriloquist's voice come out of a dummy's mouth? It doesn't! This is a trick of your senses. The human brain processes sounds and sight in the same area. When you see the dummy's mouth moving, your brain assumes any speech you hear is coming from this source. Fooled you!

Talking Heads

Hearing speech from people on TV and in the movies works on the same principle as ventriloquism. The sound of speech is coming from speakers near the screen, not the people's mouths. But your brain links sight and sound input to make you think you're hearing the image speak.

Synesthesia

The brain can play some very unusual tricks on people. **Synesthesia** is a rare condition where unrelated sensory information gets linked in the brain. People with this condition might hear or taste colors, see smells, or feel an "eyeball touch" when someone looks at them.

THINGS ON STRINGS

Yes, strings can come in quite handy. Bo Peep uses one to zip-line out of the antique store. Tugging on Woody's string activates his voice box. "There's a snake in my boot!" There are some classic toys that use strings too. So whether you pull them, bounce them, or twirl them . . . toys on strings do some amazing things!

Yo-Yo

Yo-yos are marvels of energy transfer! A still yo-yo in your hand has potential energy. As it drops or rises, it has two kinds of kinetic energy: kinetic energy of movement (up-and-down motion) and kinetic energy of **rotation** (because it is spinning on a central rod called an axle). Friction slows the yo-yo down, but you can keep it going by gently yanking the string and adding energy back into the system. Whew—that's a lot of science for one simple toy!

Falling with Style

The first time Buzz "falls with style," he is caught on a plane attached to the ceiling with a string. Around and around in circles he goes! The tension of the string exerts a force that keeps Buzz going in a circle. If the string broke, the force would vanish and he would continue flying straight ahead!

Paddleball

Paddleball toys have a rubber ball attached to an elastic string, which is attached to a wooden paddle. You hit the ball with the paddle—*WHACK!* It flies off in the opposite direction. The elastic string stretches at first, then reaches its limit. The ball stops moving—then gets yanked backward as the elastic returns to its original shape. Hit the ball again to repeat the process!

SOFT AND CUDDLY

All objects can teach us something about science, and stuffed animals like Ducky and Bunny are no exception. Let's take a peek at the science of plush.

True Love

Stuffed animals are just objects of cloth and fluff. But many children get very attached to one certain plush toy. They think of it as being real, with its own personality and thoughts. **Psychologists** call these special toys **transitional objects** or comfort objects. They comfort a child when the caregiver is not present.

Sense of Smell

Lotso smells like strawberries! How do we pick up this delicious scent? Scented toys release tiny particles called **molecules**. The molecules are sucked into our noses, where they bind with scent **receptors**. The receptors send messages to the brain, which decides what you are smelling based on the molecules' chemistry and shape.

Soft to the Touch

A fluffy teddy bear is soft to the touch and squishy when you hug it. We feel these things thanks to receptors in our skin and the underlying muscles. These receptors pick up information about pain, pressure, temperature, stretching, and itching. They send this information to the brain, where it is interpreted. You feel the delightful tickle of your teddy's fur!

cold receptor · hair · pressure receptor

pain receptor · touch receptor · touch receptor · hot receptor

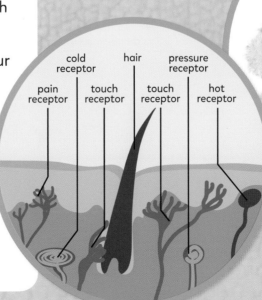

Human skin contains many kinds of touch receptors. They are different shapes, and they are found at different depths.

BOUNCING BALLS

When it comes to toys, it doesn't get much more basic—or more fun—than balls. What's the science behind the **bounce**?

Bouncy!

When a ball hits the ground, its kinetic energy has to go somewhere. Some of it goes into moving the ball's molecules around to deform the ball. Some of it turns into heat and sound, and some of it is absorbed by the surface the ball hits. The heat, sound, and transferred energy are lost, but the movement energy is not!

Because the ball is an elastic object, it springs back to its original round shape. This change pushes the ball upward, and you see a bounce.

Rubber

Many balls were originally made of **rubber**. Natural rubber comes from trees! It is harvested mostly in India and Malaysia. It starts out as a sap called **latex**. To collect the latex, tubes called taps are inserted into tree trunks. The latex runs out into buckets. It is taken to a factory and processed into dry rubber.

Super Balls

Super Balls are not made of natural materials. They are synthetic. They are made of a special material with extra-super-duper-tightly linked molecules. When a Super Ball hits the ground, it loses very little energy. Almost all the energy is transferred into movement, so the upward bounce is almost as high as the original drop.

TOYS THAT FLY

Before he learns that he is a toy, Buzz Lightyear thinks he can fly. He can't— but many toys can. Up, up, and away!

Paper Airplanes

Paper airplanes (and real airplanes too) are subject to four main forces during flight. **Thrust** is a force that produces forward motion. **Drag** is a force that resists this motion. **Lift** is a force that pushes upward on the wings to raise the airplane into the air. Gravity opposes lift and pulls the plane downward. When lift and gravity are balanced, the plane can glide a long way. If the forces are unbalanced, the plane will crash!

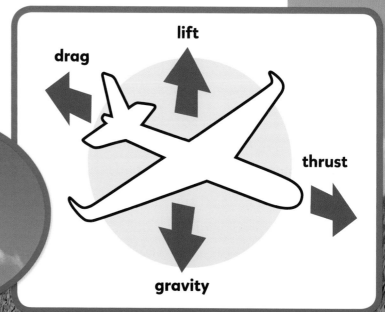

Kites

A flying kite is subject to the same four **aerodynamic** forces as an airplane. But a kite doesn't move forward, so it needs moving air—wind—to produce thrust and lift. The wind speed needed depends on the kite's weight and design.

Drones

Drones use whirling wings called **propellers** to create thrust. The speed of the propellers controls the amount of thrust. When the propellers spin very quickly, the thrust is greater than gravity, and the drone rises. When the drone reaches the desired height, the operator slows the propellers until thrust and gravity are equal. The drone hovers in place!

IN CONTROL

Throughout most of human history, the only way to control a toy was to touch it in some way. Today, technology lets us control toys like RC and other electronic items from a distance. Let's check out this super science.

Radio and Remote Control

Radio and remote control are similar, but not exactly the same. Remote control is any type of control that occurs from a distance. Instructions can be sent as electrical signals through an attached wire, or transmitted through the air via **radio waves**. If radio waves are used, that's called radio control. All radio control is remote control, but not all remote control is radio control. Got it? Good!

What Are Radio Waves?

Radio waves are part of something called the **electromagnetic spectrum**. This term describes the range of electromagnetic waves in the universe. We can't see electromagnetic waves—but if we could, they'd be sort of like waves in the ocean, with peaks and troughs. Some waves vary between up and down very quickly. These waves are said to have high frequencies. Other waves vary between up and down slowly. These waves are said to have low frequencies.

Radio waves have the lowest frequency in the electromagnetic spectrum. We can't see them or hear them—but they're there, and they can carry information.

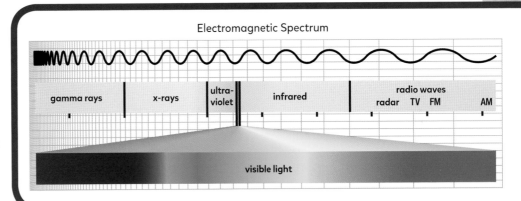

Electromagnetic Spectrum

gamma rays | x-rays | ultra-violet | infrared | radio waves — radar TV FM AM

visible light

Walkie-Talkies

Walkie-talkies are battery-powered **transceivers**. This word means they can both transmit (send) and receive signals. You push a button to activate transmission mode, then speak into the device. When you release the button, the device goes into receiver mode. Information travels between devices via radio waves.

Bluetooth

Like walkie-talkies, Bluetooth devices communicate with radio waves. They are designed to be used at very short ranges—usually 30 feet (9 m) or less. Bluetooth toys such as games, cars, and anything with a built-in speaker are usually controlled by an app on a smartphone.

CLASSIC TOY DESIGN

Toys don't just magically appear. They are carefully designed to have the perfect mix of looks, materials, and function. Many of the techniques used in this process are centuries old.

Prototypes

A **prototype** is a preliminary model of a toy. A designer may build dozens of prototypes, making small changes each time, before settling on the final model. Historically, each prototype was made by hand. The process could take years!

The Art of Design

Designing prototypes is an art! To create a new doll, for example, a team of designers hand-paints makeup onto sample heads. They sew on hair with a sewing machine, then cut and style it by hand. They try hundreds of outfits. All the prototypes are then evaluated to choose the doll's final look.

Artist styling a doll's hair

Technical Drawings

A technical drawing shows a precise image of a toy or another object with exact **proportions**. It usually shows the object from many angles. A manufacturer uses the drawing as a **blueprint** to create the object shown. It takes years of training and study to master the skill of technical drawing.

GOING HIGH-TECH

Modern technology has changed the process of toy design! Things that were once done by hand can now be done by computers. This technology makes the process faster, easier, and more accurate.

CAD

CAD stands for computer-aided design or computer-aided drafting. CAD **software** lets designers make technical drawings of toys and toy parts on a computer instead of doing them by hand. The process is faster and more precise than hand drawing.

3D Printing

Toy designers today can use **three-dimensional** (3D) printers to create sample toys and toy parts. A 3D printer works by building up objects in layers. Each layer is printed using plastic or another material. When the layer dries, another layer is added on top. This process is repeated many times to create a three-dimensional object.

Computer Animation

Computer animation software can test toys, cars, planes, and other mechanical devices before they are made! A **virtual** toy is assembled and moved around on a computer screen to make sure the parts will fit correctly and work the way they are supposed to. Only then is a real-world prototype made.

TOYS OF THE FUTURE

Classic toys like balls, dolls, and stuffed animals will never go out of style. At the same time, technology is making new types of toys possible. Let's take a look at some toys of the future!

Mind Control

You can control some toys just by thinking about what you want them to do! Mind-controlled toys come with a headset. When you concentrate, your brain produces electrical signals. The headset picks up these signals and transmits them to the toy. Mind-control technology is crude right now, but watch out—it's bound to get better, fast.

Virtual Reality

Virtual reality toys come with viewers that cover your eyes. You see computer-generated images that match motions your body is making. This creates a strong illusion that you are really doing the imaginary things you are seeing. Today virtual reality is most popular in games, but who knows what the future may bring?

Artificial Intelligence

Toys that learn are said to have **artificial intelligence**. This means they contain computers that have the ability to solve problems in a different way than a human might. Toys that talk to you and get to know you are prime examples of this technology.

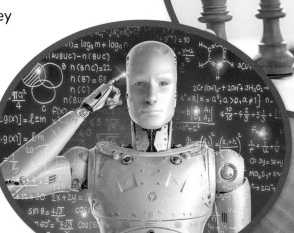

HAPPY TRAILS!

With the help of your favorite characters, you've learned a lot about the way toys work and how they are designed. You've learned a lot about science too. You can see that each and every toy, no matter how it looks or what it does, is a treasure trove of scientific knowledge. Now that you know so much, it's time to experiment. Dive into your own toy chest. Pull out your favorite toys, and watch the science from this book in action. If you have a special toy that wasn't covered, play with it and see if you can identify some of the concepts you learned. You'll see that learning science is child's play . . . for real!

GLOSSARY

aerodynamic: relating to the movement of air and other gases

anode: the terminal on a battery that gives up electrons

artificial intelligence: the ability of a machine to sense its environment and respond in a way that seems intelligent

assemble: to connect or put together the parts of something

automation: the use of machines and technology to make processes run on their own without human help

axles: bars connected to the center of a circular object such as a wheel that allows or causes it to turn

batteries: two or more single cells working together to produce electrical energy. See *cells*.

blueprint: a carefully rendered, precisely drawn design or pattern that can be followed to make something

bounce: to move quickly up, back, or away from a surface after hitting it

cathode: the terminal on a battery that receives electrons

cells: devices that store chemical energy and release it as electrical energy when activated. See *batteries*.

centrifugal force: an apparent force that draws a rotating object away from the center of rotation

ceramic: a material made of clay or similar materials and hardened by heat

circuit: a closed path that allows electricity to flow from one point to another

clockwork: a mechanism with a spring and toothed gearwheels, used to drive a mechanical clock, toy, or other device

compression: squeezing, pressing, or flattening as a result of pressure

current: the flow of electric charge, carried by moving electrons

drag: a type of friction that resists the forward movement of an object

dummies: puppets operated by a ventriloquist so they seem to be alive

elastic: tending to return to its original shape after being deformed in some way

electricity: a form of energy caused by the directional flow of electrically charged particles

electrolyte: a chemical that releases electricity-conducting ions when dissolved in water

electromagnetic spectrum: the range of wavelengths or frequencies over which electromagnetic radiation extends

electrons: particles that carry negative electrical charges

energy: the capacity or power to do work. Energy exists in many forms and can change from one form to another.

energy transfer: the conversion of one form of energy into another

evaporated: changed from a liquid form to a vapor

fibers: fine threadlike pieces of material. Fibers can be woven together to form larger objects.

forces: anything that causes a change in an object's motion

friction: a force that is created when objects rub against each other. Friction creates heat.

gravity: a force that pulls objects together. On Earth, it always pulls downward.

injection: forcing a molten material or a liquid into a cavity

joint: a place where two things or parts are joined

kaolin: a very fine, nearly white clay used to make many ceramics

kiln: a furnace or oven for burning, baking, or drying something

kinetic energy: the energy of an object in motion

latex: the sap of the rubber tree

lift: a force that pushes objects upward

magnetic: able to attract certain metals, such as iron

magnitude: a measure of size or extent

mainspring: the driving spring of a clockwork mechanism

mechanical: operated by a machine or machinery

membrane: a thin, flexible sheet of tissue

molds: hollow containers used to give shape to molten or hot liquid material (such as wax or metal) as it cools and hardens

molecules: groups of atoms bonded together to form a stable substance

molten: having changed from a solid to a liquid form by heat; melted

particles: very small bits of matter

porcelain: a type of ceramic that is smooth and hard and that usually contains a white clay called kaolin

potential energy: the stored energy that a piece of matter has because of its position or nature or because of the arrangement of its parts

pressure: a force that acts over an area rather than at a single point

propellers: mechanical devices for propelling a boat or aircraft, consisting of a spinning shaft with two or more blades attached

proportions: the relationships between one thing and another in size, amount, or degree

prototype: a preliminary model from which later forms are developed

psychologists: scientists who study the mind and emotions and their relationship to behavior

radio waves: the lowest-energy type of wave in the electromagnetic spectrum

receptors: special cells or groups of nerve endings that respond to sensory input

rotation: circular movement

rubber: a strong, waterproof, elastic substance made from the juice of a tropical tree or produced chemically

simple machines: mechanical devices that change the direction or magnitude of a force

software: programs used to do tasks on a computer

stabilize: to make steady

synesthesia: a condition in which sensory input triggers the wrong sense in addition to or instead of the correct one

synthetic: not of natural origin; created by humans through chemical processes

textiles: fabrics produced by weaving, knitting, or felting

three-dimensional: having the three dimensions of length, width, and height

thrust: a force that pushes objects forward or upward

transceivers: devices that can both transmit and receive radio waves

transitional objects: items that a child becomes very attached to and prefers above others

ventriloquists: performers who speak in such a way that the voice seems to come from another source

vibration: back-and-forth movement in a quick, regular pattern

virtual: existing only in electronic form, not in the physical world

work: force applied to an object that moves the object

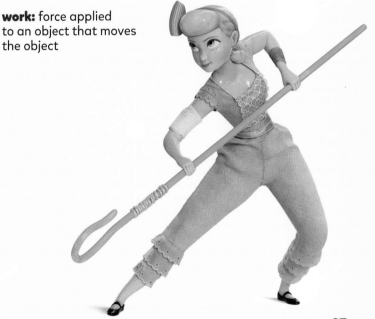

INDEX

PHOTO CREDITS